Getting Things Done

Simple Guide To Become More Productive, Stress-Free, Get More Done in Less Time, and Be Highly Effective Today

JONATHAN BRIGGS

ISBN: 0615865062
ISBN-13: 978-0615865065

XMS Publishing

1391 NW St. Lucie West Blvd
Suite 247
Port St Lucie, FL 34986

First Published, 2013

ISBN: 0615865062
ISBN-13: 978-0615865065

Published in the United States of America

DEDICATION

First and foremost this book is dedicated to God for giving me the ability to share gifts with the world. I would also like to include my ever supporting Mom. She is always there for me and always encouraged me to follow my dreams.

Contents

ACKNOWLEDGMENTS

Thank you to the following individuals who without their contributions and support this book would not have been written:

My mentor and coach Keith Dougherty, without your guidance and support I would not be where I am today.

My business partner Steve, you provide a great support system for our continued success.

Introduction

Have we ever taken any attempt to find the most important resource in our life? Maybe or maybe not, but we often seem to fall between two fires when looking for the best way to succeed in life. Taking advantage of the most advanced technology used by the search engines, we can now find what we need. With money, we can buy almost all things. However, there is still one thing that we can neither buy nor manage.

Do we know what that valuable thing is? Here is a hint, it may help us become successful or its shortage may even push through the door of failure? Yes!, It is our time that we can never stop, or direct, as we want. If we look back through the pages of history, what we might see is the game of time, which constantly makes our human civilization helpless. However, we can certainly do things to overcome such barriers, and that is to what time management mainly refers.

We all have exactly the same amount of time that can be counted as sixty seconds in a single minute, sixty minutes in each hour, 1,440 minutes in each day, and 525,600 minutes in every year. It is common that the majority of us confess faltering to grip it. It is also evident that only a few of us have successfully made the best use of their time. We may wonder how those salts of earth have managed to do all these things. The answer is very simple. Those people have been able to figure out the best ways to manage their tasks in accordance with the available time. In fact, it is no miracle that we all can achieve that if we can achieve proper skills to conduct time management.

What Does Time Management Actually Mean?

Time management is actually a set of well-organized and deliberate actions that help us form good habits eliminating the bad ones, especially those ones that simply steal our time. We cannot simply consider time management as the plan to manage our tasks with the available time. It is mainly a great set of actions that help us overcome the issues that often fail us and make us lag behind. Only a properly designed management system for our time can show us the easiest ways to go ahead amid the burdens of heavy schedules and the pangs of multitasking.

The author designed the content to convey a proper understanding of time management, its benefits and the ways we can achieve time management skills with our own efforts. Following is the list of topics that this content deals with step-by-step:

Benefits of time management

What is our time worth or the determination of the value of our time

Identifying the time suckers and getting rid of them or creating a good schedule that works

Tools for success or time management tools

The best activities to do during our new found free time

Each of the sections comes with concise but relevant discussions to help readers get the most of it.

SECTION: 1
Benefits of Time Management

The units of measuring time are equal to people of all ages and classes ranging from the powerful administrators to the aimless vagabonds and from the children to the oldest people. So, why is there a difference in human beings regarding the ability to grip time or utilize it to our needs? There must be something that contributes to the proper utilization of time and materialization of our dreams and goals. In practice, very few people can attain the benefits of proper utilization of time as most people seem to fail or end up losing the battle of time. So, what is it?It is time management that has paved the way to success for those people.

What does time management signifies?

Many successful people often consider time to be the most valuable resource while others may say it is the most undervalued resource. In practice, the two attributes are the same. Time management refers to the process of not only managing time but also controlling the most precious or undervalued resource. Time management simply means managing an individual's living existence in relation to time. Time management consists of setting priorities, managing the situation and properly utilizing every moment to one's needs. Good time management emphasizes on the elimination of the time suckers. More precisely, forming habits and following strategies that just assist the utilization of time in accordance with one's day-to-day activities are the essence of time management.

An individual should always be up and doing in order to manage his or her time and to cope with the surroundings successfully. Successful time management ensures that the individual has control of his or her time. For uninterrupted maintenance of one's work, as well as personal life with near and dear ones, it is imperative that one should have a well thought time management plan. Flexibility and ability to quickly responsed to any of the newly discovered opportunities can be in one's control if one concentrates not on how much time one finds, but on how one makes use of the available time.

Truths about time:

The concept of time management seems to be a misnomer due to its associated complexity as most people cannot manage their available time like the way they can manage other resources, such as finances, assets, manpower, information, authority, and so on. In view of experiences from our ancestors, it is almost evident that all of the above-mentioned resources can be augmented or enhanced, reduced or diminished, or transferred or controlled. It is time, which can hardly be manipulated and controlled as per our needs. Human beings can only manage themselves in relation to time.

As mentioned above, every human being has the same amount of time, or at least, the mathematical value of time is equal to everyone. Therefore, the advantages of time management can be perceived through several viewpoints. In fact, there are some of the most common advantages that people of all avenues can enjoy only if they already have some time management skills. The following are the benefits of time management perceived by students, business people, service holders, and people in general.

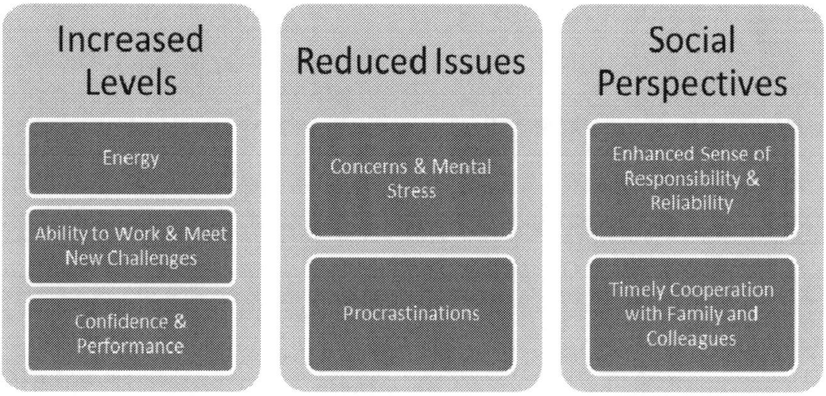

Common benefits that make people happy:

➢ *Reduction in stress levels radically:*

When we have too many tasks to carry out and too little time to employ, we simply become burdened with the thoughts of our future happening, and so, we suffer from stress. Again, repetition of such event will add to our stress level and at one point, life becomes a stress to us. However, if we can really organize all our tasks and prioritize them in order of their deadline and importance, it will be easier for us to avoid getting frustrated or stressed. We all know what ills stress can do to us if we fail to remove the notorious issue from our day-to-day life. Here lies the substantial significance of time management to fight stress.

➢ *Enhancement of productivity and opportunity:*

Proper management of time ensures that you complete all your tasks in view of their deadlines and significance. It may also happen that you are being hooked into too many commitments all of which are equally important to you. Consequently, you are likely to fall down if you do not have real capability to schedule and manage your tasks. If you each of your jobs in time, it simply means you have enough time to enjoy your leisure. It also means you have reserved time for any of your extra duties or chores. Therefore, you need not necessarily worry about your performance. This increases both your energy to do things in time and you can engage yourself in newer opportunities or activities when necessary.

- ***Health benefits:***

When you have enough time to handle your day-to-day commitments and jobs, you do have the opportunity to enjoy some time of a day on your own. You do not have concerns to pass through tight schedule that could have choked you. With adequate rest and relaxation, your brain works properly without having to being pressured due to nerve wrecking propositions. Therefore, you enjoy a good health along with a good flow of your professional tasks.

- ***Authority over most things in life:***

Assume that you have been successful in carrying out your duties and professional commitments most of the time. You have already managed to be a dependable human within your family and professional surroundings. It is simply the outcome of proper time management, which has given you pleasant authority over people around you. You can also claim to have a good control of your surroundings back into your own comfort. Your assignments can hardly dictate to you, but it is you who make things go in accordance with your demand. Now, you may take pride in you as you have proper sense of accomplishments, which increases your confidence level as well.

Managing one's time also begets some other benefits to people who are engaged in different professions like studentship, business and services. Let's take a look at them.

Students may enjoy some benefits, which are given below:

- ✓ Little chance to miss the academic deadlines
- ✓ Fewer issues to worry about: the term papers, lab reports and group assignments
- ✓ Complete preparation for the ensuing examinations and sound sleep at nights before the exams
- ✓ Assistance to make preparation for the new opportunities after post college sessions

Moreover, business people and service holders may enjoy the following benefits if they have time management skills:

- ✓ Ability to manage all official documents, interact with colleagues properly, attend the seminars and meetings
- ✓ Assistance to develop timely communications with superiors and follow all their commands
- ✓ Enough free time to share with the family and relatives and participate in social gatherings like birthday parties, marriage ceremonies, and reunions

Researchers and scientists also acknowledge the value of time managements, which are below:

- ✓ Providing required time and energy to conduct extensive research and collect valuable information
- ✓ Providing enough scope to process all findings and prepare detailed presentation

- ✓ Ability to keep abreast of new inventions and discoveries relevant to their fields of research

Time management works as the driving force to manage our tasks and avoid all confusions or multitasking concerns. To lead a healthy and organized life amid happy surroundings, the value of time management cannot be overstated. Realistically speaking, it is imperative that we all have some effective time management skills to cope with the fast changing world.

SECTION: 2

What Is Your Time Worth

There are a few things that we, the human beings, are not in possession or authority. Among such things, time is one that we can never manage, but it is our day-to-day activities and living styles that we can manage in order to cope with the ever-running chariot of time. We all should feel the compulsion that we do things as time demands. However, a good understanding of proper time management will not help us until we understand the value of our time. In fact, to ensure that we abide by a good time management system, what we have to ensure initially is that we understand the substantial significance of our time. A good understanding of the value of our own time will help us overcome many obstacles to progress. In most cases, we may find that many of us are still ignorant of how our own time is important for us to be guided by proper time management.

What misconception do people have about their time?

A common misconception about time is that time is free and takes no toll to be available for us. In practice, almost all corners of this earth will see the same kind of negligence towards time, but the reality becomes bitter when time is not properly utilized. Only then, we come to understand how much time we spend or lose. Despite the best of their efforts and hard works, many businesses or organizations, either big or small may even fall into the trap of considering time as being free. Often considered as a perpetual resource that comes free, we do not have to issue any check for our time. Some people may have the idea that they can work for three hours in a certain place and six or more hours in another place without having to spend a single penny for it.

How much valuable should you consider your time to be?

As said above, there are people who may think that their time is not worth money. Holding this belief, those people are only undervaluing themselves and wasting the most valuable of free resources. Most famous people of the world emphasized the importance of our time by demonstrating proper utilization of time can make us valuable creatures on earth. It is time that can simultaneously make us valueless.

Let's think for while about our life. Suppose that we do all our duties on time, and never waste our time doing nothing. Hence, it is very likely that we have enough opportunity to heave a sigh of relief as we are not meant to be hooked in routine-bound schedules. We have enough free time to relax and enjoy refreshment. Even if we make mistakes in any of our jobs, we can certainly correct those as we have time on hand and we are never in a hurry. When we have to beat the time, we always need to be well organized and work in a disciplined manner. We have a goal to achieve, and we have a vision to materialize. It is our time that will take us to that horizon of success if we consider its worth.

Knowing the worth of our time, we can distinguish between important and insignificant tasks. We can also figure out how much return we will receive from our tasks as we have already considered their importance. Consequently, we can cxcludc ourselves from jobs that pay low in proportion to pour time invested and look for new opportunities that suit our demand. Again, time has been the parameter.

Now, we can think about our failure to be punctual and utilize our time considering that it is worthless as it is rather free. Time always goes on and never turns back. If we fail to go with the unending trend, we are likely to fall behind. We may discover our existence amid sheer dissatisfaction of our superiors and family members, as we could not have managed anything in time that we were supposed to accomplish previously.

By dint of timely success, we can make a huge difference to our respective communities. We can stand as a reliable employee in the office or a punctual student in the school or college. Once we have managed to make use of time properly, we are also likely steer clear of others who fail to go with time. It is the proper management of our time which makes people value our time. It is our time that allows us to apply all our dormant skills and talents to bring about a change to ourselves as well as the world. Hence, we should never sell ourselves short thinking that our time is worth nothing but zero.

What the truth about time states:

It is almost evident that we do not have to offer any direct payment for money. It might be a fancy way of telling others that time is a special productivity panacea that costs nothing. However, this thinking is a trap. Based on the many experiences of our practical life, the idea about time will surely prove to be a just a trap because time does not have physical value but it is not really free. In view of practical surroundings, time signifies two things, an opportunity and a direct expense.

We may gain some ideas about how time becomes an opportunity for all of us. Our time has been giving us the opportunity to grow and become productive. With time, we leverage our skills, acquired knowledge, sharpen expertise and develop our passion.

Assume that a good fundraiser, with his or her great

communication skills has been able to score large contributions for his or her organization. The person could leverage his or her skills for a single hour. Should he or she use that single hour to stuff envelopes for the direct mail? Should the person use the hour at any networking event? If an hour of stuffing envelopes yields only $600 as donations and a networking event would ensure $1,000 as donations, by stuffing envelopes, the fundraiser has lost out on $400 of contributions.

Thus, the example above shows that the decision on where to apply our valuable time yields the opportunity of higher outcomes for our productivity. Time has made our skill set distinctive and productive.

SECTION: 3

Get Rid of the Time Suckers

Has anyone of us thought about how we pass each of our days? Probably yes, but we do not seem to realize why many of us often fail to manage our day-to-day tasks even though we have enough time and opportunity to carry them out. Will those reasons remain undisclosed until doomsday? No, this is very simple as we have several time thieves that simply take away our time and make us fall between two fires. Those are time suckers that make us go without having to think about the significance of our tasks. Some of the most common time suckers and the ways we can fight them are listed below:

Some Common Time Stealers:

- *Poor Planning*
- *Crisis Management*
- *Procrastination*
- *Interruptions*
- *Do-it-myself Attitude*
- *Unnecessary Meetings*
- *Shuffling Blues*
- *Poor Setup*
- *Poor Networking*
- *Negative Attitude*

Do we often fall a victim to poor planning?

Many of us fail to recognize the significance of proper planning and get too impatient to wait for something to be done. Consequently, the evils of improper planning are inevitable. Poor planning usually triggers erroneous advent and results in rather unproductive time utilization on some the most critical ways for our jobs to be accomplished. Gradually, things become harder than they seemed to be, and we are at a loss with the burden of our daily schedules. We should consider following the proverb that says, “Look before you leap”. We must make a plan before heading towards anything since proper planning may cost a little initially, but the consequences are really sweeter than our efforts are worth.

Are we experiencing crisis management?

With time, we get involved in multiple avenues like family, society, office and personal affairs, which require us to prioritize our tasks in order of their importance and deadline. When we fail to ensure perfect prioritization, it gives birth to its offspring called crisis management. People who undergo the pangs of crisis management are likely to fail to distinguish between their emergency schedules and unimportant tasks. We should always make a list of our doable tasks. Then, we have to arrange them in accordance with their materialistic significance, and we must avoid our emotions, as we are sure not to take the path of ultimate failure.

Are we acquainted with our internal enemy named procrastination?

Putting off our tasks for tomorrow or future is one of the most persistent habits that we form inside our person unknowingly. It really seems easy for us to put off our due tasks rather than completing them right away. Our tasks gradually pile up and may force us to run into an unbearable time crunch in the end. We call our enemy procrastination, which is usually triggered by the feeling of possible failure or success, perfectionism in all spheres and desire to do them at a time mostly in incorrect priorities. However, we should again follow a proverb that says, "Something is better than nothing". It is always better to do something than to procrastinate. We should always stand upright and take heart to carry out our mandatory tasks regardless of the possible failure or intimidating success. In addition, we should not always look for perfection, as we know mistakes or flaws are unavoidable for us. Rather, we should focus on the objectives if it is possible to gain.

Are we offended by interruptions?

When we cannot concentrate on our jobs and exercise proper control over the surroundings, we have to struggle. However, the most likely reason for it is the interruptions or distractions that develop from improper planning. Interruptions are some of the avoidable thieves which often take away our valuable time in different forms like drop-in visitors or guests, unwanted telephones, unimportant e-mails, undetermined or unscheduled meetings, ineffective communications and confusing chain of command. So, how should we approach interruptions? We can handle all frequent distractions and interruptions by being aware of what we are to do in every 24-hour time. We need to remember our schedule. Trying to be centralized will be easier if we choose to work in such an environment not exposed to noise and crowd.

Feeling of 'do-it-myself':

Most people somehow go with a feeling that others cannot do what they can do. Many managers or administrators feel their inferior employees are not able to work as fairly as they can. They are often afraid of the fact that things may go wrong if handled by others. Such feeling also stops even the most capable managers or homemakers from materializing long term plans because those people are likely bogged down in their daily operations. However, good time management suggests that we do share our tasks in accordance with the requirements, and we should also have a belief in someone else's ability, but we must check to see if the particular individual really has the ability to do that.

Do we attend unnecessary meetings frequently?

When working in our offices, we might attend a meeting that does not have a specific agenda. We can expect nothing productive of it. Therefore, it is certainly an unnecessary meeting. These meetings are just thieves as our valuable working time is wasted without any accomplishment. We should always be mindful of each of our meetings and conversations that are goal driven and likely to deliver some outcomes.

Being in a mess with the 'shuffling blues':

Disorganization of our working tools and elements often lead to our tasks going astray. Keeping necessary things in an easily accessible place, removing clutter and following a detailed day-planner will help us stay away from the *shuffling blues*. It is essential for all of us to get things in place since we should not waste our working time looking for the essentials here and there just when we start working for the day.

Do we have a poor interior setup?

We always like to have our interior setup based on our personal preferences in case of both our offices and homes. At times, our personal choices might be in conflict with the most practical necessity, and we often make mistakes when setting up our households or offices. Consequently, finding things or retrieving items when necessary takes most of our time. Therefore, we have to keep things within our easy reach for which we need to have a systematic interior setup. It will help us avoid wearing out the carpets or misplacing our furniture to retrieve things like keys, papers, pen drive and other small items.

What type of networking we are accustomed to, poor or excellent?

It is always recommended that we manage to develop a good networking so that we can deal with the people around us effectively. Poor networking at offices results in a failure as managers cannot coordinate their tasks and cooperate with their stuff and colleagues to complete things in a timely manner. It may happen that the manager has already ordered some of his or her employees to complete anything within a time crunch schedule, but the concerned employees could not respond in time. Hence, a complete dissatisfaction among the official employees is inevitable and the entire surroundings may become unfriendly. That is why, building a good network among all our people is imperative to manage our time efficiently.

Do we have a positive attitude?

Nothing sinks our days more effectively and radically than having a bad attitude. It causes us to dwell on the issues instead of the solutions and makes us throw a full working day without progression. Therefore, we must stop finding faults or complaints against others. We should always have a positive attitude towards others as an environment that consists in perfect cooperation and understanding always begets expected results and saves our time and efforts.

In addition to the mentioned time stealers, we may be hooked in some other time wasters, which include the following:

- ✓ *Enjoying TV programs frequently*
- ✓ *Going through newspapers or magazines excessively*
- ✓ *Idle chat or gossip on telephone*
- ✓ *Checking mails frequently*
- ✓ *Answering to unwanted or unknown telephone calls*
- ✓ *Meetings*
- ✓ *Paying utility bills standing on a long queue*
- ✓ *Day-dreaming*
- ✓ *Fretting over multiple personal affairs*
- ✓ *Frequently caught in traffic snarls*
- ✓ *Planning on change things by fits and starts*
- ✓ *Waiting for any positive results instead of working*
- ✓ *Taking naps unnecessarily*
- ✓ *Habit of eating various snacks between every meal*
- ✓ *Drinking slowly*
- ✓ *Smoking frequently*
- ✓ *Shopping without any specific choice*
- ✓ *Wagering assets or money*

We must be up and doing to avoid all time suckers that only waste our valuable time. Following the facts and suggestions of good time management skills, we can certainly go a long way in our day-to-day life and career as well.

SECTION: 4

Tools for Success

In the previous sections, we have learned about the significance of proper time management and its widespread impact on each sphere of our life. Many of us seem to have been confident about the way they claim to manage their time and accomplish all their tasks efficiently and timely. The irony of fact is that the truth still dwells far beyond their reach. However, several tools that have a proven track record of success in assisting people with their crucial concerns about time management. In the following lines, some of the best effective time management tools are discussed in brief.

An 'Activity Log' can be the best tool to manage our time:

Commonly known as Activity Diary, an Activity Log or a Job Activity Log. Do we know what an *activity log* actually is? It is a written record of ways we should spend our time to ensure proper utilization of our time to bring success.

This activity report enables us to track each change in our energy level, overall alertness and regular effectiveness throughout our day-to-day life. It will also help us eliminate activities that are of low value and simply steal our valuable time. Thus, keeping an activity diary can be a great way to enhance our productivity.

How to prepare and keep an activity log:

We can open up a fresh spreadsheet to set up the column headers as shown below:

- ✓ Date/Time
- ✓ Description of our activity
- ✓ How we feel
- ✓ Duration
- ✓ Value (whether high or medium or low or none)

This is a typical template of an Activity Log

Date/Time	*Activity Description*	*How You Feel*	*Duration*	*Value*

The To-do Lists to prioritize our tasks in order of importance for successful accomplishments:

Due to the lack of proper coordination and poor time management, we often get overwhelmed to see the amount of pending tasks we still need to do. Missing deadlines and failing ourselves frequently lead us to the way of sheer frustration and stress. One of the most crucial reasons for this unwanted existence is our failure to arrange our tasks in order of their actual importance.

Creating a To-Do List will help us overcome the issue of managing our important tasks. A well-planned to-do list shows our tasks in accordance with their priority.

How to create a well-organized To-Do List:

Creating a to-do list is simple when we are knowledgeable about the significance of our jobs.

We have to write down all our tasks properly, and we should break out our first action step and mark it as the larger task if our tasks are large. Write down all of the tasks that you need to complete.

We should run through our tasks by allocating relevant priorities from A as very important to F as unimportant. In case of having too many tasks as high priority issue, we can again demote the less important tasks among those high priority tasks.

This is a simple template of a typical To-do List

TASKS	***A (Very Urgent)***	***F (Less Urgent or Important)***

Technology for our wellbeing:

We are fortunate enough to live in an age of technological advancement, which has also brought to us a plethora of some amazing tools that ease out all our confusions and hesitation. Following is the list of some of the greatest technological tools that have been very popular among people who tend to come out successful in this age of globalization where everyone is busy with many commitments.

A List of the Latest Technological Tools for Success

- ✓ *YadaHome Family Organizer*
- ✓ *Toggl, The Remember Everything Tool*
- ✓ *Evernote*
- ✓ *ZOMM Personal Concierge*
- ✓ *Google Calendar*
- ✓ *NowDo This*
- ✓ *Checkvist*
- ✓ *Lastpass*
- ✓ *WakeupOnStandby*

SECTION: 5

I Have All This Time, Now What

Time is one of the few things that is valuable and on the constant move. As said earlier, we cannot manipulate or make time go after the passage of a desired duration; we always have to count on time. However, human life, being dynamic, may experience sudden changes that can open up certain amount of free time, which we were not previously aware we had. Is it the time for us to put off our thoughts for tomorrow or pass moments just for relaxation or idleness? Probably not, just because of the duties and responsibilities, we have hardly enough time to focus on our near and dear ones and ourselves. This can be the most precious time of our life which we can utilize to bring some refreshments to our entire surroundings by doing creative and deliberate activities that should focus on the wellbeing of our individuality.

Filling our newfound free time with some of the most effective pursuits can be a good way of enhancing our innate creativity, physical and mental energy, enthusiasm, and a true sense of achievements. If we can manage to use our free time in a productive manner, we can certainly overcome our deep-rooted inability to enjoy relaxation since we might be afraid of 'just doing nothing'. Having some good ways to enjoy and utilize our free time can be highly beneficial to us, and it will help us to fulfill our common desire to be well-rounded, to be fully engaged in life, and to be an efficient as well as productive individual.

To get started with the whole thing, we must have to think profoundly as it is not something that only requires us to do things and enjoy the free time on our hand. We have to follow some specific ideas to make our plan, and then, we should find some good options to choose, which we will put into action during our free time. Following are some of the greatest suggestions about how to deal with our newfound free time and the way we can adopt to make it a success:

Factors to consider before starting anything:

Making a good plan to utilize free time:

Free time does not necessarily mean that we have all easy thoughts to make it effective. We should have the ability to use our free time in the way we would like. Our initial plan to utilize our newfound free time should accordingly focus on what we like most and consider being worthy.

We need to create a to-do list that shows all tasks we want to do. The list should not be filled with such activities that only bring monotony. Again, we should not always focus on the productivity only since we are going to enjoy the time as effectively as possible. Our main goal is to be happy with our time and gain something that was quite unreachable during our routine-bound life. We can also consider creating a colorful visualization board that should set out the certain ways in which we can utilize our future free time.

Averting notorious stressors:

As we all want our newfound free time to be highly enjoyable, we should not allow things of our busy time to bleed into it. If we fail to stop our regular mundane activities from creeping into our free time in the apparent pretense of making it *useful*, we are sure to lose the spirit of gaining anything from the free time. Again, we will have the very flexible boundaries between our free time and working time, thereby wasting our free time.

List of Don'ts during free time

- ✓ Usual tasks or household chores
- ✓ Answering all emails and sending voice messages
- ✓ Watching TV for a long time
- ✓ Some sorts of constant actions like meeting colleagues regarding official issues
- ✓ Just keep playing with electronics to lose the sense of free time with the *gamer brain*
- ✓ Catching up on work time
- ✓ Getting hooked in internet time

Going ahead with some of the best ideas to utilizing our newfound free time:

Expanding our comfort zone:

If we step beyond our regular comfort zone, our free moments will become a great journey for our self-discovery and growth. In addition, expansion of our comfort zone will also help us to feel interested in sparking our innate curiosity and broadening our overall awareness. We can also try to do things that we could not manage to do. We should also learn to say "no" when necessary to expand our comfort zone and to enjoy ourselves.

Trying to use media creatively:

Many of us have some good skills regarding editing or creating visual presentation. We can create a video that focuses on our personal passions and emotions on how we consider the world. We can also write down all our ideas using the power of words.We can also find online sites that allow people to build up their online portfolio by doing some creative and constructive works. We can certainly indulge this new approach to our media usage.

Taking part in voluntary avenues:

We can volunteer in certain occasions or events, which can be a big way to give something back to our society or community. Regardless of experiences and skills, voluntary jobs are available, and we have many options to choose. We can meet new people and are acquainted with many unknown aspects of our society if we go trying to be part of any of the voluntary organizations that serve humanity in times of distress. This is a great chance for us to rise above the level of humanity.

Learning only to gain pleasure and to learn:

Some of us would think that learning beyond academic necessity or professional avenues is a mere waste of time and energy. However, it is a great mistake since we can certainly embellish our souls with what we have kept away so far for fear for losing grades, professional restrictions and tight schedules. We have to keep in mind that this is our free time and we must do something that assuages our soul and enriches our mind. Many of us would have fancied ourselves being engaged in archaeology, dancing in ballroom, making jewelry with aesthetic designs, first aid for wilderness, or hang-gliding. With time, most of these passions seem to be lost away in the undisclosed path of life. Accordingly, in our free time we can immerse ourselves into learning any of these things that would once make us feel thrill in our conscious mind. Now, we are free of stress, as we do not have to achieve certain goals.

Concentrating on our spirituality:

In our free time, we can go undertaking all spiritual works, as it is time for us to give ourselves adequate space to unwind amazingly, reflect thoroughly, and think profoundly about the most realistic picture and the purpose of our existence. Regardless of our state, being religious or not' spiritual time is said to be one of the most essential time for us to be a real human. It is the way to undergo self-effacement, self-denial and self-judgment. We can meditate, join, or even return to our particular religious places like a church, a synagogue, a mosque, or a temple.

Some exclusive ideas showing what to do during new found free time:

- We can indulge our individual hobby or pastime more sincerely.
- We can turn some of our household activities like cooking and gardening into a source of joys and refreshments other than considering as only chores.
- Our free time can be best valued if we consider downsizing or reorienting our lifestyle to bring a new but positive twist. For example, we can consider taking part in some home improvement projects.
- Most of us have a pet who we love very much. It is high time we spent some more time with our loving pets.
- Our free time can also be considered as the best time to build new connection with our neighbors or old friends who are just living distant without any communication. Being friendly with people around us will help us create a good networking to improve our social state in terms of cooperation, solidarity and friendship.

Conclusion

We Have Learned All about Time Management, Now What?

We have to acknowledge the truth that every second of our life is equally important if we have a proper understanding of its value for the success that we desire. We have to make sure that we are not sitting idle after learning all essentials about time management process. As our life is a continuous process that involves several turns and twists, we have to be up and doing to concentrate on what we have in our mind. Certainly, hardly anyone dislikes success in life. Time management goes hand-in-hand with our overall prosperity.

Suppose that we have managed to arrange each of our essential things within our reach. So, are we going to be successful anyway? No, it does not necessarily ensure that we are sure to succeed unless we can be consistent with our new resource, of time management skills.

We should not look back when we are trying to go ahead. Many of us may get discouraged when we fail several times despite all our deliberate efforts and trials to achieve our respective goals. Failure is often considered as one of our biggest enemies that stands in the way to our success; however, proper time management does not recommend that we remain silent or inactive after recurrent failure. Rather, the best thing we can do is go ahead, considering our failure as the power to make things happen.

Cooperation with our intimates can be a big way to achieve the skills of time management. We can take heart when we see one of our colleagues or friends has managed to be successful in his or her way of life by following the same way of managing his or her tasks in relation with time.

In addition, it is always a good way for us to interact with people around us regarding the way we are trying to lead our everyday life by virtue of proper utilization of time. Once we have been successful in handling our official duties and household tasks, we may not experience the pangs of deadline failure, less productivity and procrastination. These are the evils of our life that we can hardly cope with in the absence of time management.

To be a reliable human being, we must be productive and punctual. As we all like to be praised by our colleagues and relations, we have a little opportunity to escape what time requires us to do.

We have to remember, ***"Every moment of our life on earth is the gift that our Creator has given us to sustain"***.

Again, ***"Time can be considered as the ticket to the greatest show on earth"***.

We must not forget that we are just separate creations of our Creator as we are gregarious, and we certainly have some duties to the people we are closely associated with us. This is how time management can make it easier for us to pay the debt to our family or offices or our own life in general.

Resources

My other book **Power of HABIT**:

Inside Discover..

- How to Replace Bad Habits with a Healthy New Lifestyle
- Why you have a better chance of freeing yourself from a bad habit by taking responsibility for your own program
- Why most successful self-changers fail at least once before they succeed
- Why willpower alone isn't enough
- Why quitting a habit cold turkey usually doesn't work
- And a lot more!

Go here now or find it on Amazon:

http://www.kd7.co/jbpower

Made in United States
Troutdale, OR
11/03/2026

56847387R10031